05

Vanishing Rain Forests

RAIN FORESTS TODAY

Ted O'Hare

This plantation has replaced a rain forest.

Rourke
Publishing LLC
Vero Beach, Florida 32964

www.rourkepublishing.com

PHOTO CREDITS: All photos ©Lynn M. Stone

Editor: Frank Sloan

Cover and page design by Nicola Stratford

Library of Congress Cataloging-in-Publication Data

O'Hare, Ted, 1961-
  Vanishing rain forests / Ted O'Hare.
      p. cm. -- (Rain forests today)
  Includes bibliographical references (p.   ) and index.
  ISBN 1-59515-156-7 (hardcover)
  1. Rain forest ecology--Juvenile literature. 2. Rain forests--Juvenile literature. 3.
Deforestation--Tropics--Juvenile literature. I. Title. II. Series: O'Hare, Ted, 1961-
Rain forests today.
  QH541.5.R270434 2004
  333.75'13--dc22

                                                    2004006059

Printed in the USA

CG/CG

Table of Contents

Where the Rain Forests Are   5

Vanishing World   6

Cutting the Forests Down   11

Forest to Farm   14

Rain Forests and Weather   16

The Greenhouse Effect   18

Useful Rain Forests   20

Update   22

Glossary   23

Index   24

Further Reading   24

Websites to Visit   24

Where the Rain Forests Are

Tropical rain forests grow in the warm lands on or near the **equator**. The biggest rain forest is in South America. Brazil has nearly one-third of the world's tropical rain forests.

West Africa, Southeast Asia, and Central America all have tropical rain forests. There are also smaller rain forests in Mexico, in Australia, and on islands in the Caribbean Sea and the South Pacific Ocean.

The rain forest once on this hill has been cleared for a cattle pasture.

Vanishing World

Tropical rain forests are wonderlands of many **species** of plants and animals. Scientists believe that more than half of the species in the world live in rain forests.

Many of these plants and animals are not known. And, unfortunately, some of them may never be known. They are disappearing along with the rain forests themselves.

Cattle have taken the place of wild rain forest animals on this Central American farm.

Ocelots have become rare in the
South and Central American rain forests.

Some of these species may not live anywhere else in the world. And some of the plants and animals that have never been studied won't be around. Plants and animals that become **extinct** can never be replaced.

Scientists believe that as many as 150 species a day may be disappearing. This comes out to 50,000 species a year!

Many rain forest animals, like this golden lion tamarin of South America, are in danger of extinction.

Rain forests have poor soil, so this farm, once forest, will produce crops for only a few years.

Cutting the Forests Down

Large amounts of rain forests are being cut down, bulldozed, or burned. Why?

Many tropical countries need open land. Because of this, rain forests are being destroyed to make room for farms, crops, cattle, roads, and homes.

Rain forests are cut and burned for farms.

Brauillo Carillo National Park,
Costa Rica, is a protected rain forest.

Most of the remaining tropical rain forests are not **protected**. Sometimes huge parts of rain forests are destroyed by **logging**. A country can make money quickly by selling its rain forest trees for lumber.

Sometimes only some of the trees in a rain forest are cut down. The rest are left standing.

Many rain forests are cut down for the lumber made from their trees.

Forest to Farm

Many nations with rain forests cut them down to make farm land. People need space to grow crops. Grazing cattle or growing coffee beans can now be found on land that was once rain forest.

But land that was once rain forest rarely makes good farmland. The soil is not very rich, or **fertile**. After just a few years, the soil is not very good for growing crops.

Once rain forest, this land is now a fruit-growing farm.

Rain Forests and Weather

Tropical rain forests are moist and have high **humidity**. This moisture escapes into the earth's **atmosphere**. Moisture in the atmosphere is healthy. Destroying the rain forests may harm the earth's weather.

Light rain falls in a lush rain forest.

Morning mist shows a rain forest's high humidity.

The Greenhouse Effect

Many scientists believe the earth's atmosphere is becoming too warm. They believe heat is being trapped in the atmosphere, just like in a greenhouse. This warming of the atmosphere is known as the Greenhouse Effect.

Burning rain forests may cause the atmosphere to warm. If the earth gets hot enough, ice at the poles could begin to melt. Sea levels might rise dangerously.

Cutting forests reduces moisture and helps heat the earth's atmosphere.

This open Central American countryside was once thick rain forest.

Useful Rain Forests

A healthy rain forest is good for everyone. The forest plants help keep the air clean. They keep air temperatures steady. The roots of the plants keep soil in place. Otherwise the soil would **erode** and cause dirty streams.

Rain forests support an amazing number and variety of living things.

Rain forest leaves shine in an April shower.

Update

Every second 2.4 acres (1 hectare) of tropical rain forest are destroyed. This is the same as two football fields! Each year 78 million acres (31 million hectares) of rain forest are destroyed throughout the world. This is an area larger than the European country of Poland.

And when a **habitat** is destroyed, animals, plants, and people disappear.

Glossary

atmosphere (AT muss feer) — the "blanket" of air around the earth

equator (ee KWAY tur) — the line drawn on maps around the earth's middle

erode (ee RODE) — to eat into or wear away

extinct (EK stinkt) — no longer existing

fertile (FUR til) — able to grow plants easily

habitat (HAB uh tat) — a special area in which plants and animals live

humidity (hu MID uh tee) — wetness or moisture in the air

logging (LOG ging) — cutting down trees for lumber

protected (pro TECKT ed) — kept safe in some way

species (SPEE sheez) — a certain kind of plant or animal within a closely related group

Index

Australia 5
Brazil 5
Caribbean Sea 5
Central America 5
equator 5
farmland 14
Greenhouse Effect 18

habitat 22
humidity 16
logging 13
Mexico 5
South America 5
Southeast Asia 5
West Africa 5

Further Reading

Chinery, Michael. *Resources and Conservation*. Crabtree, 2001.
Moore, Eva. *The Magic School Bus in the Rain Forest*. Scholastic, 2000.
Morgan, Sally. *Saving the Rainforests*. Franklin Watts, 1999.

Websites to Visit

www.rainforest-alliance.org/resources/what.html
www.rainforesteducation.com/index.htm
www.ran.org

About the Author

Ted O'Hare is an author and editor of children's nonfiction books. He divides his time between New York City and a home upstate.